Beach Life
Coloring Book

An Adult Coloring Book Featuring Fun and
Relaxing Beach Vacation Scenes, Peaceful Ocean
Landscapes and Beautiful Summer Designs

an Imprint of **The Fruitful Mind Publishing LTD.**
www.coloringbookcafe.com

Have questions? Let us know.
support@coloringbookcafe.com

 facebook.com/coloringbookcafe    @coloringbookcafe

This Book
Belongs To:

BONUS

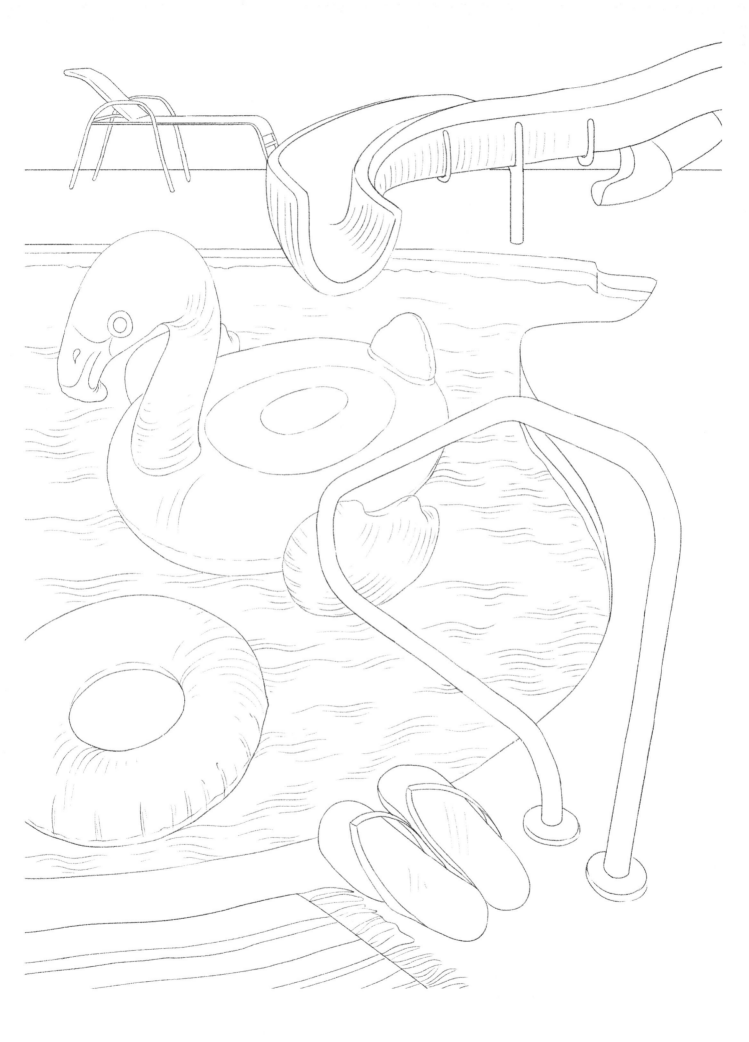

Made in the USA
Coppell, TX
15 April 2020

20051942R00031